MOURNING DIARY

ALSO BY ROLAND BARTHES

A Barthes Reader
Camera Lucida
Critical Essays
The Eiffel Tower and Other Mythologies
Elements of Semiology
Empire of Signs
The Fashion System
The Grain of the Voice
Image-Music-Text
Incidents
The Language of Fashion
A Lover's Discourse
Michelet
Mythologies
The Neutral
New Critical Essays
On Racine
The Pleasure of the Text
The Preparation of the Novel
The Responsibility of Forms
Roland Barthes by Roland Barthes
The Rustle of Language
Sade / Fourier / Loyola
The Semiotic Challenge
S/Z
Writing Degree Zero

MOURNING DIARY

October 26, 1977–September 15, 1979

ROLAND BARTHES

TEXT ESTABLISHED AND ANNOTATED BY NATHALIE LÉGER

TRANSLATED FROM THE FRENCH BY RICHARD HOWARD

HILL AND WANG

A DIVISION OF FARRAR, STRAUS AND GIROUX

NEW YORK

Hill and Wang
A division of Farrar, Straus and Giroux
18 West 18th Street, New York 10011

Printed in the United States of America
Originally published in French in 2009 by Seuil, France, as *Journal de Deuil*
Published in the United States in 2010 by Hill and Wang
First American paperback edition, 2012

A portion of this book first appeared, in slightly different form, in *The New Yorker*.

Unless noted otherwise, the pictures featured in this edition come from the author's private collection. The pictures of Roland Barthes in his mother's arms as an infant and as a child, the picture of his mother in Biscarosse, and the picture of the family house in Urt were originally published in *Roland Barthes by Roland Barthes*. The index cards come from the original manuscript of *Mourning Diary*. They are reproduced here with the kind authorization of Michel Salzedo, Roland Barthes's stepbrother and literary executor.

The Library of Congress has cataloged the hardcover edition as follows:
Barthes, Roland.
[Journal de deuil. English]
Mourning diary : October 26 1977–September 15 1979 / Roland Barthes ; text established and annotated by Nathalie Léger ; translated by Richard Howard.—1st ed.
p. cm.
Includes bibliographical references.
ISBN: 978-0-8090-6233-1 (alk. paper)
1. Barthes, Roland—Diaries. 2. Linguists—France—Diaries. 3. Critics—France—Diaries. 4. Bereavement. I. Léger, Natalie. II. Howard, Richard. III. Title.

P85.B33A3 2010
410.92—dc22
[B]

2010005775

Paperback ISBN: 978-0-374-53311-3

Designed by Jonathan D. Lippincott

www.fsgbooks.com

20 19 18 17 16 15

CONTENTS

Editor's Note • *vii*

Foreword by Nathalie Léger • *ix*

Mourning Diary • 1

October 26, 1977–June 21, 1978

Continuation of the Diary • 153

June 24, 1978–October 25, 1978

Further Diary Pages • 211

November 4, 1978–September 15, 1979

Some Undated Fragments • 245

Some Notes on *Maman* • 249

Afterword by Richard Howard • 257

EDITOR'S NOTE

In his diary, Roland Barthes refers to a wide range of works. The references that may seem cryptic to the reader are explained in a footnote. For the sake of chronological consistency, we have listed the French edition of the works Barthes alludes to, copies of some of which could be found in his library at the time when he was writing his diary of mourning. We have referred to an English edition in parentheses whenever one is available.

FOREWORD
by Natalie Léger

The day after his mother's death, October 25, 1977, Roland Barthes began a "mourning diary." He wrote in ink, sometimes in pencil, on slips of paper (regular typing-paper cut into quarters) of which he kept a constant supply on his desk.

While writing this diary, Barthes prepared his Collège de France course on "The Neutral" (February–June 1978), wrote the text of his lecture "For a Long Time I Would Go to Bed Early" (December 1978), published many articles in various journals and magazines, wrote *Camera Lucida* between April and June 1979, drafted several pages for his project "Vita Nova" during the summer of 1979, and prepared his double course at the Collège de France on "La Préparation du roman" (December 1978–February 1980). At the root of each of these major works, all explicitly placed under the sign of his mother's death, are the notes of *Mourning Diary*.

These notes were for the most part written in Paris and in Urt, near Bayonne, where Barthes occasionally stayed with his brother, Michel, and the latter's wife, Rachel. He made several trips during this period, notably to

Morocco, which Barthes, regularly invited there to teach, enjoyed visiting. Preserved at IMEC, *Mourning Diary* is presented here in its entirety, note by note. We have corrected the chronological order of the notes as it had evidently been distorted. The format of the quartered pages required an always concise wording, but some notes are written on both sides of the paper, and occasionally the text continues on the front of several notes. The initials provided by the author designate his intimates and have been preserved as written. The brackets are the author's; a few footnotes are provided to explain the context or clarify an allusion.

Henriette Binger was born in 1893. At twenty she married Louis Barthes; a mother at twenty-two, she was a war widow at twenty-three. She died at the age of eighty-four.

The reader is presented not with a book completed by its author, but the hypothesis of a book desired by him, which contributes to the elaboration of his œuvre and, as such, illuminates it.[1]

1. This edition could not have been completed without the kind assistance of Bernard Comment and Éric Marty.

MOURNING DIARY

October 26, 1977–June 21, 1978

October 26, 1977

First wedding night.
But first mourning night?

October 27

—You have never known a Woman's body!

—I have known the body of my mother, sick and then dying.

October 27

Every morning, around 6:30, in the darkness outside, the metallic racket of the garbage cans.

She would say with relief: the night is finally over (she suffered during the night, alone, a cruel business).

As soon as someone dies, frenzied construction of the future (shifting furniture, etc.): futuromania.

October 27

Who knows? Maybe something valuable in these notes?

—SS: I'll take care of you, I'll prescribe some calm.

—RH: You've been depressed for six months because you knew. Bereavement, depression, work, etc.—But said discreetly, as always.

Irritation. No, bereavement (depression) is different from sickness. What should I be cured of? To find what condition, what life? If someone is to be born, that person will not be *blank*, but a *moral* being, a subject of *value*—not of integration.

October 27

Immortality. I've never understood that strange, Pyrrhonic position; I just don't know.

October 27

Everyone guesses—I feel this—the degree of a bereavement's intensity. But it's impossible (meaningless, contradictory signs) to measure how much someone is afflicted.

October 27

—"Never again, never again!"

—And yet there's a contradiction: "never again" isn't eternal, since you yourself will die one day.

"Never again" is the expression of an immortal.

October 27

Overcrowded gathering. Inevitable, increasing futility. I think of her, in the next room. Everything collapses.

It is, here, the formal beginning of the big, long bereavement.

For the first time in two days, the *acceptable* notion of my own death.

October 28

Bringing *maman*'s body from Paris to Urt (with JL and the undertaker): stopping for lunch in a tiny trucker's dive, at Sorigny (after Tours). The undertaker meets a "colleague" there (taking a body to Haute-Vienne) and joins him for lunch. I walk a few steps with Jean-Louis on one side of the square (with its hideous monument to the dead), bare ground, the smell of rain, the sticks. And yet, something like a savor of life (because of the sweet smell of the rain), the very first discharge, like a momentary palpitation.

October 29

How strange: her voice, which I knew so well, and which is said to be the very texture of memory ("the dear inflection . . ."), I no longer hear. Like a localized deafness . . .

October 29

In the sentence "She's no longer suffering," to what, to whom does "she" refer? What does that present tense mean?

October 29

A stupefying, though not distressing notion—that she has not been "everything" for me. If she had, I wouldn't have written my *work*. Since I've been taking care of her, the last six months in fact, she *was* "everything" for me, and I've completely forgotten that I'd written. I was no longer anything but desperately hers. Before, she had made herself transparent so that I could write.

October 29

In taking these notes, I'm trusting myself to the *banality* that is in me.

October 29

The desires I had before her death (while she was sick) can no longer be fulfilled, for that would mean it is her death that allows me to fulfill them—her death might be a liberation in some sense with regard to my desires. But her death has changed me, I no longer desire what I used to desire. I must wait—supposing that such a thing could happen—for a new desire to form, a desire following her death.

October 29

The *measurement* of mourning.

(Dictionary, Memorandum): eighteen months for mourning a father, a mother.

October 30

At Urt: sad, gentle, *deep* (relaxed).

October 30

. . . that this death fails to destroy me altogether means that I want to live wildly, madly, and that therefore the fear of my own death is always there, not displaced by a single inch.

October 30

Many others still love me, but from now on my death would kill no one.

—which is what's new.

(But Michel?)

October 31

I don't want to talk about it, for fear of making literature out of it—or without being sure of not doing so—although as a matter of fact literature originates within these truths.

October 31

Monday, 3:00 p.m.—Back alone for the first time in the apartment. How am I going to manage to live here all alone? And at the same time, it's clear there's no other place.

October 31

Part of me keeps a sort of despairing vigil; and *at the same time* another part struggles to put my most trivial affairs into some kind of order. I experience this as a *sickness*.

October 31

Sometimes, very briefly, a blank moment—a kind of numbness—which is not a moment of forgetfulness. This terrifies me.

October 31

A strange new acuity, seeing (in the street) people's ugliness or their beauty.

November 1

What affects me most powerfully: mourning in layers—a kind of sclerosis.

[Which means: no depth. Layers of surface—or rather, each layer: a totality. Units]

November 1

Moments when I'm "distracted" (speaking, even having to joke)—and somehow going dry—followed by sudden cruel passages of feeling, to the point of tears.

Indeterminacy of the senses: one could just as well say that I have no feelings or that I'm given over to a sort of external, feminine ("superficial") emotivity, contrary to the serious image of "true" grief—or else that I'm deeply hopeless, struggling to hide it, not to darken everything around me, but at certain moments not able to stand it any longer and "collapsing."

November 2

What's remarkable about these notes is a devastated subject being the victim of *presence of mind*.

November 2

(Evening with Marco)
I know now that my mourning will be *chaotic.*

November 3

On the one hand, she wants everything, total mourning, its absolute (but then it's not her, it's I who is investing her with the demand for such a thing). And on the other (being then truly herself), she offers me lightness, life, as if she were still saying: "but go on, go out, have a good time . . ."

November 4

The idea, the sensation I had this morning, of the offer of lightness in mourning, Eric tells me today he's just reread it in Proust (the grandmother's offer to the narrator).

November 4

Last night, for the first time, dreamed of her; she was lying down, but not ill, in her pink Uniprix nightgown . . .

November 4

Today, around 5:00 in the afternoon, everything is just about settled: a definitive solitude, having no other conclusion but my own death.

Lump in my throat. My distress results in making a cup of tea, starting to write a letter, putting something away—as if, horribly enough, I *enjoyed* the now quite orderly apartment, "all to myself," but this enjoyment *adheres* to my despair.

All of which defines the *lapse* of any sort of work.

November 4

Around 6 p.m.: the apartment is warm, clean, well-lit, pleasant. I make it that way, energetically, devotedly (enjoying it *bitterly*): henceforth and forever I am my own mother.

November 5

Sad afternoon. Shopping. Purchase (frivolity) of a tea cake at the bakery. Taking care of the customer ahead of me, the girl behind the counter says *Voilà*. The expression I used when I brought *maman* something, when I was taking care of her. Once, toward the end, half-conscious, she repeated, faintly, *Voilà* (*I'm here*, a word we used to each other all our lives).

The word spoken by the girl at the bakery brought tears to my eyes. I kept on crying quite a while back in the silent apartment.

That's how I can grasp my mourning.

Not directly in solitude, empirically, etc.; I seem to have a kind of ease, of control that makes people think I'm suffering less than they would have imagined. But it comes over me when our love for each other is torn apart once again. The most painful point at the most abstract moment . . .

November 6

The comfort of Sunday morning. Alone. First Sunday morning without her. I undergo the week's daily cycle. I confront the long series of times without her.

November 6

I understood (yesterday) so many things: the unimportance of what was bothering me (settling in, comfort of the apartment, gossip and even sometimes laughter with friends, making plans, etc.).

My mourning is that of the loving relation, not that of an organization of life. It occurs in the words (words of love) that come to mind . . .

November 9

I limp along through my mourning.

Constantly recurring, the painful point: the words she spoke to me in the breath of her agony, the abstract and infernal crux of pain that overwhelms me ("My R, my R"—"I'm here"—"You're not comfortable there").

—Pure mourning, which has nothing to do with a change of life, with solitude, etc. The mark, the void of love's relation.

—Less and less to write, to say, except this (which I can tell no one).

November 10

People tell you to keep your "courage" up. But the time for courage is when she was sick, when I took care of her and saw her suffering, her sadness, and when I had to conceal my tears. Constantly one had to make a decision, put on a mask, and that was courage.

—Now, *courage* means the *will to live* and there's all too much of that.

November 10

Struck by the *abstract* nature of absence; yet it's so painful, lacerating. Which allows me to understand *abstraction* somewhat better: it is absence and pain, the pain of absence—perhaps therefore love?

November 10

Embarrassed and almost guilty because sometimes I feel that my mourning is merely a susceptibility to emotion.

But all my life haven't I been just that: *moved*?

November 11

Solitude = having no one at home to whom you can say: I'll be back at a specific time or who you can call to say (or to whom you can just say): *voilà,* I'm home now.

November 11

Horrible day. More and more wretched. Crying.

November 12

Today—my birthday—I'm feeling sick and I can no longer—I no longer need to tell her so.

November 12

[Stupid]: listening to Souzay* sing: "My heart is full of a terrible sadness," I burst into tears.

*whom I used to make fun of.[1]

1. See "The Bourgeois Art of Song" in *Mythologies,* 1957 (Hill and Wang, 1972; revised, 2012).

November 14

In a sense I resist the Invocation to the Status of the Mother in order to explain my distress.

November 14

One comfort is to see (in letters I've received) that many readers had realized what she was, what we were, by her mode of presence in "RB."[1] Hence I had succeeded in that, which becomes a present achievement.

1. *Roland Barthes by Roland Barthes*, 1975 (Hill and Wang, 1977; revised, 2010).

November 15

There is a time when death is an *event*, an ad-venture, and as such mobilizes, interests, activates, tetanizes. And then one day it is no longer an event, it is another *duration*, compressed, insignificant, not narrated, grim, without recourse: true mourning not susceptible to any narrative dialectic.

November 15

I am either lacerated or ill at ease
and occasionally subject to gusts of life

November 16

Now, everywhere, in the street, the café, I see each individual under the aspect of ineluctably *having-to-die,* which is exactly what it means to be *mortal.*—And no less obviously, I see them as *not knowing this to be so.*

November 16

Sometimes roused by desires (say, the trip to Tunisia); but they're desires of *before*—somehow anachronistic; they come from *another shore*, another country, the country of before.—Today it is a flat, dreary country—virtually without water—and paltry.

November 17

(Fit of depression)

(because V. writes me that she still sees *maman*, in Rueil, *dressed in gray*)

Mourning: a cruel country where *I am no longer afraid.*

November 18

Not to *manifest* mourning (or at least to be indifferent to it) but to *impose* the *public* right to the loving relation it implies.

November 19

[Status confusion]. For months, I have been her mother. It is as if I had lost my daughter (a greater grief than that? It had never occurred to me.)

November 19

To see with horror as quite simply possible the moment when the memory of those words she spoke to me would no longer make me cry . . .

November 19

A trip from Paris to Tunis. A series of airplane breakdowns. Endless sojourns in airports among crowds of Tunisians coming home for Aïd Kebir. Why does the ominous effect of this day of breakdowns suit mourning so well?

November 21

Confusion, defection, apathy: only, in snatches, the image of writing as "something desirable," haven, "salvation," hope, in short "love," joy. I imagine a sincerely devout woman has the same impulses toward her "God."

November 21

Always that painful (because enigmatic, incomprehensible) wrench between my ease in talking, in taking an interest, in observing, in living as before, and the impulses of despair. Additional suffering: not to be more "disorganized." But perhaps then I'm just suffering from a preconception.

November 21

Since *maman*'s death, a sort of digestive weakness—as if I were suffering precisely where she took the greatest care of me: food (though for months she no longer prepared it herself).

November 21

Now I know where Depression comes from: rereading my diary of this summer,[1] I am both "charmed" (lured) and disappointed; hence writing at its best is merely a mockery. Depression comes when, in the depths of despair, I cannot manage to save myself by my attachment to writing.

1. Barthes published several pages of this diary from summer 1977 in *Tel Quel*, no. 82, winter 1979.

November 21
evening

"I'm bored wherever *I* am"

November 23

Grim evening at Gabès (windy, black clouds, hideous bungalows, "folklore" performance in the Hotel Chems bar): I can no longer take refuge in my thoughts: neither in Paris nor traveling. No escape.

November 24

My astonishment—and what is really my anxiety (my indisposition) comes from what, in fact, is not a lack (I can't describe this as a lack, my life is not disorganized), but a *wound*, something that has harmed love's very heart.

November 25, 1977

+ spontaneity

What I'm calling *spontaneity*: merely that *extreme* state in which *maman*, from the depths of her weakened consciousness, ignoring her own suffering, tells me, "You're not comfortable there, the way you're sitting" (because I'm sitting on a stool to fan her).

November 26

What I find utterly terrifying is mourning's *discontinuous* character.

November 28

To whom could I put this question (with any hope of an answer)?

Does being able to live without someone you loved mean you loved her less than you thought . . . ?

November 28

A cold winter night. I'm warm enough, yet I'm alone. And I realize that I'll *have to* get used to existing quite *naturally* within this solitude, functioning there, working there, accompanied by, *fastened to* the "presence of absence."

November 29

Review my notes for *The Neutral.*[1] Oscillation (The Neutral and the Present).

1. A reference to Barthes's exhaustive notes for his course on "The Neutral" given at the Collège de France (February 18, 1977–June 3, 1978). The references here are to the figures "The Active of the Neutral" and "Oscillation." Barthes's lectures are available in English as *The Neutral* (Columbia University Press, 2007).

November 29

→ "Mourning"

Explained to AC, in a monologue, how my distress is chaotic, erratic, whereby it resists the accepted—and psychoanalytic—notion of a mourning subject to time, becoming dialectical, wearing out, "adapting." Initially this mourning of mine has taken nothing away—on the other hand, it doesn't wear out in the slightest.

—To which AC responds: that's what mourning is. (He thereby constitutes it as a subject of Knowledge, of Reduction) —"That's what bothers me most. I can't endure seeing my suffering being *reduced*—being *generalized*—(à la Kierkegaard): it's as if it were being stolen from me.[1]

1. "Once I speak, I express generality, and if I refrain from speaking no one can understand me." Søren Kierkegaard, *Fear and Trembling*. Roland Barthes frequently referred to this text.

November 29

→ "Mourning"

[Explained to AC]

Mourning: not diminished, not subject to erosion, to time. Chaotic, erratic: *moments* (of distress, of love of life) as *fresh* now as on the first day.

The subject (which I am) is only *present*, not only *at present*. All of which is ≠ psychoanalysis: very nineteenth century: philosophy of Time, of displacement, modification by Time (the cure); organicism.

cf. Cage.[1]

1. The "present" is one of the basic elements of the investigations of the composer John Cage. See notably Cage's interviews with Daniel Charles in *For the Birds*, a French translation of which was in Barthes's library.

November 30

Don't say *Mourning*. It's too psychoanalytic. I'm not *mourning*. I'm suffering.

November 30

Vita nova,[1] as a radical gesture: (discontinuous—necessity of discontinuing what previously continued on its own momentum).

Two contradictory paths are possible:
1) Liberty, Hardness, Truth
(To reverse what I had been)
2) Laxness, Charity
(To stress what I had been)

1. This desire for a *vita nova*, a radically new life longed for by the mourning for the dear departed, explicitly refers to Dante's procedure, the invention by his *Vita Nova* of a poetic and narrative form in order to express love and mourning. During the summer of 1979, Barthes would sketch, under the title *Vita Nova*, a project in which the mother, *maman*, would be one of the essential protagonists.

November 30

At each "moment" of suffering, I believe it to be the very one in which for the first time I *realize* my mourning.

In other words: totality of intensity.

December 3

[Emilio's dinner with FM Banier]

Gradually I abandon the conversation (suffering because the others might suppose I am doing so for reasons of contempt). FMB (supported by Youssef) embodies a strong (and ingenious) *system* of values, codes, seductions, styles; but even as the system gains in *consistency*, I feel excluded from it. And little by little I cease struggling, I withdraw, without concern for how I appear to the others. Thus it begins by an initially slight disaffection for sociability which becomes quite radical. As it develops, it gradually combines with a nostalgia for what remains living for me: *maman*. And ultimately I fall into an *abyss* of suffering.

December 5

[The feeling I am losing JL—that he is distancing himself from me]. If I were to lose him, I would be implacably dismissed, reduced to *the region of Death*.

December 7

Now, from time to time, there unexpectedly rises within me, like a bursting bubble: the realization that *she no longer exists, she no longer exists,* totally and forever. This is a flat condition, utterly unadjectival—dizzying because *meaningless* (without any possible interpretation).

A new pain.

December 7

The (simple) words of Death:

—"It's impossible!"

—"Why, why?"

—"Forever"

etc.

December 8

Mourning: not a crushing oppression, a jamming (which would suppose a "refill"), but a painful availability: I am *vigilant*, expectant, awaiting the onset of a "sense of life."

December 9

Mourning: indisposition, a situation *with no possible blackmail.*

December 11

In the darkest part of this silent Sunday morning:

Now gradually rises within me the grim (desperate) theme: from now on, what meaning can my life have?

December 27, 1977

Urt

A violent crying jag.

(something to do with the butter, the butter dish, involving Rachel and Michel). 1) Pain of having to live with *another* "household." Everything here in Urt brings me to *her* household, *her* house. 2) Every (conjugal) couple forms a unit from which a single person is excluded.

December 29, 1977

The *indescribableness* of my mourning results from my failure to hystericize it: continuous and extremely peculiar indisposition.

January 1, 1978

Urt, intense and continuous suffering; constant sense of abrasion. Mourning intensifies, deepens. At first, strangely, I felt a sort of interest in exploring the new situation (solitude).

January 8

Everyone is "extremely nice"—and yet I feel entirely alone. ("Abandonitis").

January 16, 1978

Very few notations—but: distress—continuous discomfort interrupted by suffering (intense, today. Impossible to write this kind of discomfort).

Everything pains me. The merest trifle rouses a sense of abandonment.

I'm impatient with other people, their will to live, their universe. Attracted by a decision to withdraw from everyone [no longer bearing the world of Y.]

January 16, 1978

My universe: flat. Nothing echoes here—nothing crystallizes either.

January 17, 1978

Last night, nightmares: *maman* suffering from various indispositions.

January 18, 1978

The Irremediable is what tears me apart and what contains me (no hysterical possibility of *blackmail* with suffering, since that's over and done with).

January 22, 1978

I have not a desire but a need for solitude.

February 12, 1978

Difficult feeling (unpleasant, discouraging) of a *lack of generosity*. It troubles me.

I can only put this into some relation with the image of *maman*, so perfectly generous (and she used to tell me: you have a good heart).

I had supposed that once she was gone I would sublime that absence by a sort of perfection of "kindness," the surrender of all kinds of nastiness, jealousy, narcissism. And I am becoming less and less "noble," "generous."

February 12, 1978

Snow, a real snowstorm over Paris; strange.

I tell myself, and suffer for it: she will never again be here to see it, or for me to describe it for her.

February 16, 1978

This morning, more snow, and *lieder* broadcast on the radio. How sad!—I think of the mornings when I was sick and didn't go to school, and when I had the joy of staying with her.

February 18, 1978

Mourning: I've learned that it was immutable and sporadic: *it does not wear away*, because it is not continuous.

If the interruptions, the giddy leaps toward something else come from a worldly distraction, an importunity, depression only increases. But if these "changes" (which account for what is sporadic) make for silence, inwardness, the wound of mourning shifts toward a higher realm of thought. *Triviality* (of hysteria) ≠ *Nobility* (of Solitude).

February 18, 1978

I had thought that *maman*'s death would make me someone "strong," acceding as I might to worldly indifference. But it has been quite the contrary: I am even more fragile (unsurprisingly: for no reason, a state of abandon).

February 21, 1978

[Bronchitis. First illness since *maman*'s death.]

This morning, thought continually of *maman*. Nauseous sadness. Nausea of the Irremediable.

March 2, 1978

The thing that lets me endure *maman*'s death resembles a certain possession of freedom.

March 6, 1978

My overcoat is so dreary that I know *maman* would never have tolerated the black or gray scarf I always wear with it, and I keep hearing her voice telling me to wear a little color.

For the first time, then, I decide to wear a colored scarf (Scotch plaid).

March 19, 1978

M. and I feel that paradoxically (since people usually say: Work, amuse yourself, see friends) it's when we're busy, distracted, sought out, *exteriorized*, that we suffer most. Inwardness, calm, solitude make us less miserable.

March 20, 1978

It is said (according to Mme Panzera[1]) that Time soothes mourning—No, Time makes nothing happen; it merely makes the *emotivity* of mourning pass.

1. Probably the widow of Charles Panzera, who died on June 6, 1976, at the age of eighty; Barthes and his friend Michel Delacroix had taken singing lessons from him in the early 1940s.

March 22, 1978

When suffering, when mourning goes into its cruising speed . . .

March 22, 1978

Emotion (emotivity) passes, suffering remains.

March 23, 1978

Learning the (terrible) separation of emotivity (which diminishes) from mourning, from suffering (which is *present*).

March 23, 1978

My haste (constantly verified in recent weeks) to regain the freedom (now rid of delays) of getting to work on the book about Photography, in other words, to integrate my suffering with my writing.

Belief and, apparently, verification that writing transforms for me the various "stases" of affect, dialectizes my "crises."

—Wrestling: written, no further need to go see it
—Japan: ditto
—Olivier crisis > *On Racine*
—RH crisis > *Lover's Discourse*
[—Perhaps *Neutral* → Transformation of the fear of Conflict?][1]

1. Summing up the argument of his course on "The Neutral," Barthes will specify some weeks later: "a definition of the realm of the Neutral: any inflection that avoids or thwarts meaning's paradigmatic, oppositional structure and consequently seeks suspension of the conflictual *données* of discourse." In the May 6, 1978, lecture he writes: "Ways of evading the conflictual, 'taking a tangent' (this is really the whole course)."

Wrestling: see *Mythologies*; Japan: see *Empire of Signs*, published in France in 1970 (Hill and Wang, 1982). *On Racine* appeared in 1963 (Hill and Wang, 1964), *A Lover's Discourse* in 1977 (Hill and Wang, 1978; revised, 2010).

March 24, 1978

Suffering, like a stone . . .
(around my neck,
deep inside me)

March 25

Yesterday, explained to Damisch that emotivity passes, suffering remains—He tells me: No, emotivity returns, you'll see.

Last night, nightmare: *maman* lost. I am overwhelmed, on the verge of tears.

April 1, 1978

Actually, as a matter of fact, always that: *as if* I were *as one* dead.

April 2, 1978

What have I to lose now that I've lost my Reason for living—the Reason to fear for someone's life.

April 3, 1978

"I suffer from *maman*'s death."

(An approach to reach the literal fact)

April 3

Despair: the word is too theatrical, a part of the language.

A stone.

April 10, 1978

Urt. William Wyler's film *The Little Foxes,* with Bette Davis.

—At one point the daughter mentions "rice powder."

—All my early childhood comes back to me. *Maman.* The rice-powder box. Everything is here, present. *I am here.*

→ *The self never ages.*

(I am as "fresh" as in the "rice-powder" days)

Around April 12, 1978

Written to be remembered? Not to remind *myself*, but to oppose the laceration of forgetting *as it reveals its absolute nature.* The—prompt—"no trace remaining," anywhere, in anyone.

Necessity of the "Monument."

Memento illam vixisse.[1]

1. Remember that she lived.

April 18, 1978
Marrakesh

Now that *maman* is no more, I no longer have that impression of freedom I had on my trips (when I would leave her for short periods of time).

Mourning

Gardet
Mystique, 24[1]

[Vacillations, Fade-outs, shadow of the wing of the Definitive]

(India)

= "clear affirmation of a radical apophasis, the way of a lived intellectual *nescience*."

—the Fade-outs of Mourning = *Satori* (v. p. 42)

"devoid of all mental fluctuation"

("collapse any subject-object distinction")

1. Louis Gardet, *La Mystique*, 1970.

It was during this trip to Morocco that Barthes underwent, on April 15, a spell of vertigo analogous "to the illumination experienced by Proust's narrator at the end of *Time Regained*." This illumination is at the heart of the *Vita Nova* project (cf. note for November 30, 1977, on page 74) and of Barthes's course on "La Préparation du Roman."

Mourning *Casablanca, April 21, 1978*

Thinking of *maman*'s death: sudden and fugitive vacillations, brief fade-outs, poignant though somehow empty embraces, their essence the certainty of the Definitive.

Mourning

Casablanca
April 27, 1978
morning of my
return to Paris

—Here, for two weeks, I continually thought of *maman* and suffered over her death.

—Doubtless in Paris there is still *the house*, the system I had when she was there.

—Here, far away, every system collapses. Which causes me, paradoxically, to suffer much more when I am "outside," far from "her," among pleasures (?), "distractions." The more the world tells me, "You have everything here by which to forget," the less I forget.

Mourning

Casablanca
April 27, 1978

—After *maman*'s death I believed there would be a sort of liberation in kindness, she surviving all the more intensely as a model (Figure) and I liberated from the "fear" (of bondage) that is at the source of so much paltry meanness (since henceforth, isn't everything indifferent to me? Is not indifference (to oneself) the condition of a sort of kindness?).

—But it is, alas, the contrary that occurs. Not only do I abandon none of my egoisms, my little attachments, I continue to put myself first, to prefer myself at every turn, unable to invest lovingly in any other being; it is they who are indifferent to me, even the dearest among them. I suffer—and this is truly painful—"hardness of heart"—acedia.

Henriette Barthes, circa 1903. (© Fonds Roland Barthes/ Archives IMEC)

Henriette Barthes holding Roland Barthes as a baby in Cherbourg, 1916.

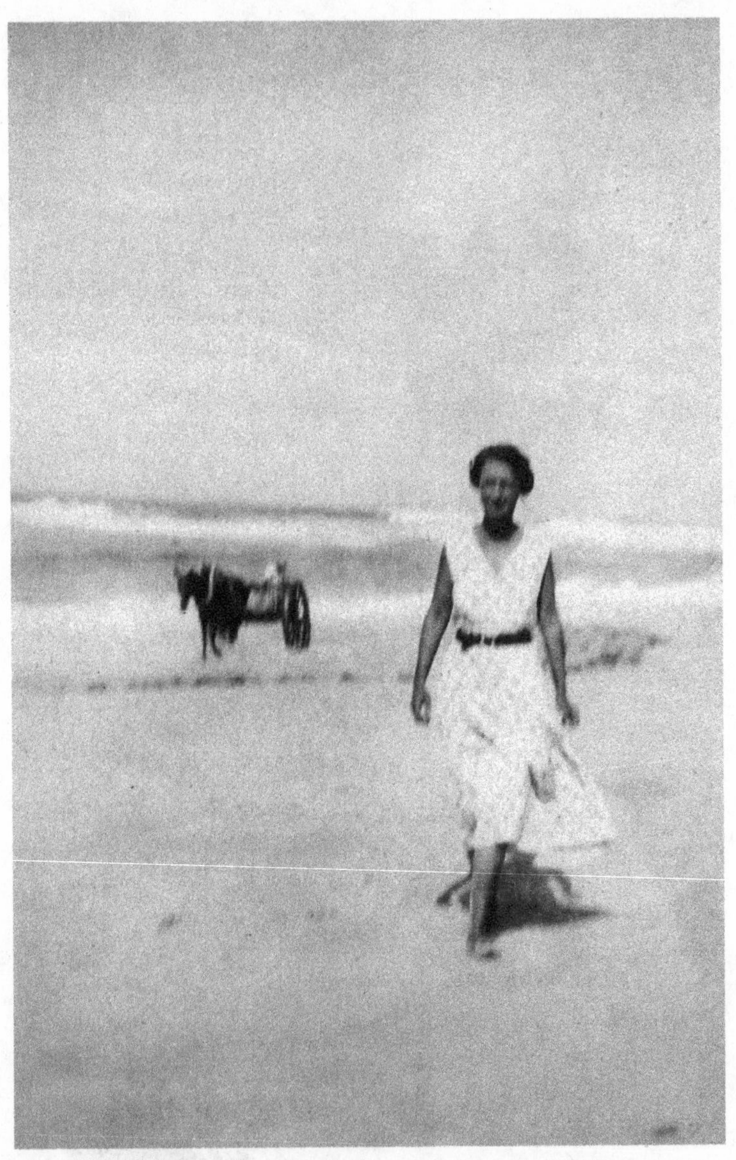

Henriette Barthes in Biscarosse, Landes, circa 1932.

Roland Barthes and his mother in Bayonne, circa 1923.

Roland Barthes with his mother and brother
in Biscarosse, Landes, circa 1932.

The family house in Urt.

Roland Barthes's mother near Chantaco, in the Basque Country.

(© Fonds Roland Barthes/Archives IMEC)

Roland Barthes in Paris, April 25, 1979. (© François Lagarde)

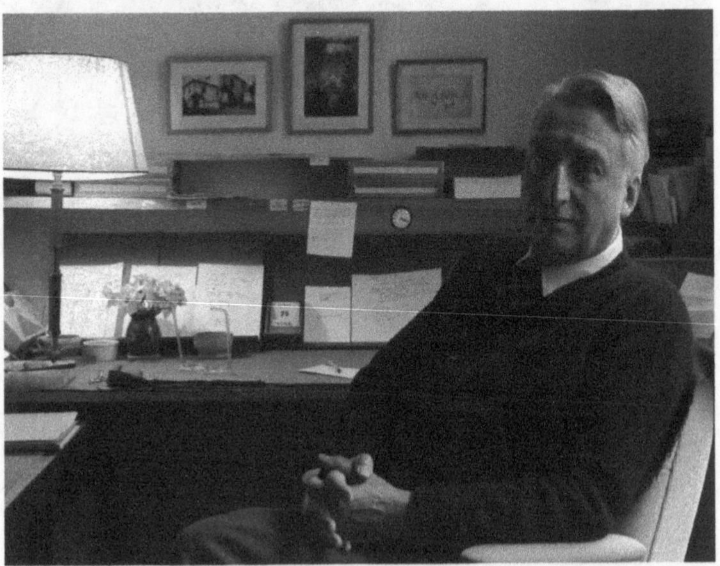

Roland Barthes at his desk in Paris, April 25, 1979. On the wall, three frames: the house in Urt (left, reproduced in this edition); a picture of camels (right); and the picture of Barthes's mother at age five in the Winter Garden (center). This last photograph is discussed in *Camera Lucida*. (© François Lagarde)

27 oct

— "Jamais plus, jamais plus!"

— Et pourtant, contradiction: ce "jamais plus" n'est pas éternel puisque vous mourrez vous même un jour. "Jamais plus" est un mot d'immortel.

Diary entry from October 27, 1977 (translation appears on page 11).

10 Nov

Frappé par la nature *abstraite* de l'absence; et cependant, c'est brûlant, déchirant. D'où je comprends mieux l'*abstraction*: elle est absence et douleur, douleur de l'absence — peut être donc amour?

Diary entry from November 10, 1977 (translation appears on page 42).

10 Nov

Gêné et presque culpabilisé parce que (parfois) je crois que mon deuil se réduit à une émotivité.

Mais toute ma vie n'ai-je été que cela : ému ?

Diary entry from November 10, 1977 (translation appears on page 43).

17 Sept 78

Depuis la mort de mam. malgré — ou à travers — effort acharné pour mettre en oeuvre un grand projet d'écriture, altération progressive de la confiance en moi — en ce que j'écris.

Diary entry from September 17, 1978 (translation appears on page 200).

May 1, 1978

To think, to know that *maman* is dead *forever, completely* ("completely," which is inconceivable without violence and without one's being able to abide by such a thought at length), is to think, letter by letter (literally, and simultaneously), that I too will die *forever and completely*.

There is then, in mourning (in this kind of mourning, which is mine), a radical and *new* domestication of death; for previously, it was only a *borrowed* knowledge (clumsy, had from others,[1] from philosophy, etc.), but now it is *my* knowledge. It can *hardly* do me any more harm than my mourning.

1. The handwriting is uncertain here: the last phrase might be read as "had from the arts."

May 6, 1978

Today—already in a bad mood—a moment, toward the end of the afternoon, of terrible sadness. A fine bass aria from Handel's *Semele (*act III) makes me cry. I think of *maman*'s words ("My R, my R").

May 8, 1978

(Readying for the day when I can finally write)

At last! Separated from that writing in which I put my very breath, where I *caught my breath* from suffering, by a thousand and one bothersome importunities, at last—

(separated from my suffering by the others, separated by them from "Philosophizing")

I held out my arms not to the image but to the philosophizing [of] that image.[1]

1. RB ultimately crossed out the preposition "of"; it is bracketed here in order to offer the reader both meanings successively envisioned by the author.

May 10, 1978

For the last few nights, images—nightmares during which I see *maman* sick, abused. Terror.

I am suffering from *the fear of what has happened.*

Cf. Winnicott: fear of a breakdown *that has occurred.*[1]

1. Donald Woods Winnicott, "La crainte de l'effondrement," *Nouvelle revue française de psychanalyse,* no. 11, 1975. This is the French translation of "Fear of Breakdown," which was written ca. 1963 and is collected in *Psycho-Analytic Explorations* (Harvard University Press, 1989).

May 10, 1978

The solitude in which *maman*'s death leaves me, leaves me alone in the realms where she had no presence: in those of my work. I cannot read attacks (wounds) concerning such realms without feeling lamentably more alone, more abandoned than before: collapse of the Recourse to which, even if it was there, I never appealed directly.

Exhaustive (panic) metonymy of Mourning, of Abandonment.

May 12, 1978
Mourning

I waver—in the dark—between the observation (but is it entirely accurate?) that I'm unhappy only by moments, by jerks and surges, sporadically, even if such spasms are close together—and the conviction that *deep down, in actual fact*, I am *continually*, all the time, unhappy since *maman*'s death.

May 17, 1978

Last night, a stupid, gross film, *One Two Two*.[1] It was set in the period of the Stavisky scandal, which I lived through. On the whole, it brought nothing back. But all of a sudden, one detail of the décor overwhelmed me: nothing but a lamp with a pleated shade and a dangling switch. *Maman* made such things—around the time she was making batik. All of her leaped before my eyes.

1. *One, Two, Two: 122, rue de Provence*, 1978, directed by Christian Gion.

May 18, 1978

Like love, mourning affects the world—and the worldly—with unreality, with importunity. I resist the world, I suffer from what it demands of me, from its demands. The world increases my sadness, my dryness, my confusion, my irritation, etc. The world depresses me.

May 18, 1978

(yesterday)

From the terrace of the Flore, I see a woman sitting on the windowsill of the bookstore La Hune; she is holding a glass in one hand, apparently bored; the whole room behind her is filled with men, their backs to me. A cocktail party.

May cocktails. A sad, depressing sensation of a seasonal and social stereotype. What comes to my mind is that *maman* is no longer here and life, stupid life, continues.

May 18, 1978

Maman's death: perhaps it is the one thing in my life that I have not responded to neurotically. My grief has not been hysterical, scarcely visible to others (perhaps because the notion of "theatralizing" my mother's death would have been intolerable); and doubtless, more hysterically parading my depression, driving everyone away, ceasing to live socially, I would have been less unhappy. And I see that the non-neurotic is not good, not the right thing at all.

May 25, 1978

When *maman* was living (in other words, in my whole past life) I was neurotically in fear of losing her.

Now (this is what mourning teaches me) such mourning is so to speak the only thing in me which is not neurotic: as if *maman*, by a last gift, had taken neurosis, the worst part, away from me.

May 28, 1978

The truth about mourning is quite simple: now that *maman* is dead, I am faced with death (nothing any longer separates me from it except time).

May 31, 1978

How *maman* is present in all I have written: in that there is everywhere a notion of the Sovereign Good.

(see the article on me by JL and Eric M. in the *Encyclopaedia Universalis*)

May 31, 1978

It's not solitude I need, it's anonymity (the anonymity of work).

I transform "Work" in its analytic meaning (the Work of Mourning, the Dream-Work) into the real "Work"—of writing.)

for:

the "Work" by which (it is said) we emerge from the great crises (love, grief) cannot be liquidated hastily: for me, it is *accomplished* only in and by writing.

June 5, 1978

Each subject (this appears ever more clearly) acts (struggles) to be "*recognized.*"

For me, at this point in my life (when *maman* is dead) I was *recognized* (by books). But strangely—perhaps falsely?—I have the obscure feeling, now she's no longer here, that I must gain recognition all over again. This cannot be by writing any book: the idea of *continuing* as in the past to proceed from book to book, course to course, immediately struck me as mortiferous (this I saw *to my dying day*).

(Whence my present efforts of resignation).

Before resuming *sagely and stoically* the course (quite unforeseen moreover) of the work, it is necessary for me (I feel this strongly) to write this book around *maman.*

In a sense, therefore, it is as if I had *to make* maman *recognized.* This is the theme of the "monument"; but:

For me, the Monument is not *lasting*, not *eternal* (my doctrine is too profoundly *Everything passes*: tombs die too), it is an act, an action, an *activity* that *brings* recognition.

(June 7. Exhibition "Cézanne's Last Years,"[1] *with AC)*

Maman: like Cézanne (the late watercolors). Cézanne's blue.

1. The exhibition Cézanne, the Last Years was held in the Grand Palais in Paris from April 20 to July 23, 1978.

June 9, 1978

By love FW is ravaged, suffers, remains prostrated, inattentive to all demands, etc. Yet he has lost no one. The being whom he loves continues to live, etc. And I, beside him, listening to him, apparently calm, attentive, present, as if something *infinitely more serious* had not occurred to me.

June 9, 1978

This morning, walking through Saint-Sulpice, whose simple architectural vault delights me; to be *in* architecture—I sit down for a moment; a sort of instinctive "prayer": that I finish the *Photo-Maman* book. And then I notice that I am always asking for something, wanting something, always pulled ahead by childish Desire. One day, to sit in the same place, to close my eyes and ask for nothing . . . Nietzsche: not to pray, to bless.

Is it not to this that mourning should lead?

June 9, 1978

(Mourning)
Not Continuous, but Immobile.

June 9, 1978

We feel the need to create a sort of *harmony* between what the dear departed has been and what is offered after that being's death: *maman* buried at Urt, her grave, and her belongings in the rue de l'Avre.[1]

1. On the rue de l'Avre, in the 15th arrondissement, lived a Protestant pastor, a friend of the Barthes family, to whom Henriette Barthes's belongings were donated for his church's charitable foundation.

June 11, 1978

Afternoon with Michel, sorting *maman's* belongings.

Began the day by looking at her photographs.

A cruel mourning begins again (but had never ended).

To begin again without resting. Sisyphus.

June 12, 1978

During the entire mourning period, of Grief (so intense that: I can't go on, I'll never get over this, etc.), continued to function, imperturbably (as if they were not properly brought up) habits of flirtations, attractions, a whole discourse of desire, of *I-love-you*—which moreover collapse very quickly—and begin again with someone else.

June 12, 1978

An onset of grief. I cry.

June 13, 1978

Not to suppress mourning (suffering) (the stupid notion that time will do away with such a thing) but to change it, transform it, to shift it from a static stage (stasis, obstruction, recurrences of the same thing) to a fluid state.

June 13, 1978

[M's fit of anger yesterday evening. R's complaints.]

This morning, painfully returning to the photographs, overwhelmed by one in which *maman*, a gentle, discreet little girl beside Philippe Binger (the Winter Garden of Chennevières, 1898).[1]

I weep.

Not even the desire to commit suicide.

1. This photograph is at the heart of the second part of *Camera Lucida*.

June 13, 1978

People's insistence (in this case, dear Severo) spontaneously to define mourning by phenomena: You're dissatisfied with your life?—Not at all, my "life" is all right, no phenomenal lack; but without any external difficulty, without "incidents," an absolute lack: this, precisely, is not "mourning," but pure *suffering*—without substitutes, without symbolization.

June 14, 1978

(Eight months after): second mourning.

(June 15)

Everything began all over again immediately: arrival of manuscripts, requests, people's stories, each person mercilessly pushing ahead his own little demand (for love, for gratitude): no sooner has she departed than the world deafens me with its *continuance*.

June 15, 1978

Strange: cruel suffering and yet—through the episode of the Photographs—the sensation that the *real mourning* is beginning (also because the screen of false tasks has collapsed).

June 16, 1978

In a conversation with Cl. M. about my anguish at seeing the photos of *maman*, envisaging a labor starting from these photos: she tells me: that may be premature.

So, always the same *doxa* (with the best intentions in the world): mourning will *ripen* (in other words, time will make it fall like fruit from the tree, or burst like a boil).

But for me, mourning is immobile, not subject to a *process*: nothing is *premature* in respect to it (so I tidied the apartment, on returning from Urt: about which someone might have said: it's premature).

June 17, 1978

1st mourning
false liberty

2nd mourning
desolate liberty
deadly, without
worthy occupation

June 20, 1978

In me, life struggles against death (the discontinuity and so to speak the ambiguity of mourning) (which will win?)—but for the moment a *stupid* life (trivial involvements, trivial interests, trivial encounters).

The dialectical problem is that the struggle leads to an *intelligent* life, not a screen-life.

June 21, 1978

Reread for the first time this mourning diary. Tears each time there was any question of her—of her person—not of me.

So emotivity returns.
Fresh as on the first day of mourning.

CONTINUATION OF THE DIARY

June 24, 1978–October 25, 1978

June 24, 1978

Virtually no signs of an internalized mourning.

This is the fulfillment of absolute internalization. All *judicious* societies, however, have prescribed and codified the externalization of mourning.

Uneasiness of ours insofar as it denies mourning.

(July 5)

(Painter II, p. 68[1])

Mourning / Suffering

(Death of the Mother)

Proust speaks of *suffering*, not *mourning* (a new, psychoanalytic word, one that distorts).

1. George D. Painter, *Proust: The Later Years* (Little, Brown, 1965). Barthes refers to the French translation by Georges Cattaui and R. P. Vial, *Marcel Proust, Volume 2, 1904–1922, Les Années de Maturité*, Mercure de France, 1966.

(July 6, 1978)
Painter II, p. 405

Autumn 1921

Proust nearly dies (overdose of veronal).

—Céleste: "We'll all meet in the Valley of Jehosephat.

—Ah! Do you really believe there's a chance of meeting? If I were sure of meeting Maman again, I'd die right away."

July 9, 1978

Leaving the apartment for the trip to Morocco, I remove the flower left on the spot where *maman* was ill—and once again the horrible fear (of her death) overwhelms me: cf. Winnicott: how true: *the fear of what has happened*. But stranger still: *and cannot recur*. Which is the very definition of the *definitive*.

Moulay Bou Selham[1]

Seeing the swallows flying through the summer evening air, I tell myself, thinking painfully of *maman*: how barbarous not to believe in souls—in the immortality of souls! the idiotic truth of materialism!

1. Moulay Bou Selham is a town in Kénitra Province, Gharb-Chrarda-Béni Hssen, Morocco.

Mourning
RTP II, 769[1]

[the mother after the grandmother's death]
". . . that incomprehensible contradiction of memory and nothingness."

1. Marcel Proust, *À la Recherche du Temps Perdu*, tome II, Gallimard, "Bibliothèque de la Pléiade," 1956. (*In Search of Lost Time*, vol. 2, Penguin Classics, 2003.)

Mourning *July 18, 1978*
(Casablanca)

Dreamed of *maman* again. She was telling me—O cruelty!—that I didn't really love her. But I took it calmly, because I was so sure it wasn't true.

The idea that death would be a kind of sleep. But it would be horrible if we had to dream eternally.

(And this morning, her birthday. I always gave her a rose. Bought two at the little market of Mers Sultan and put them on my desk)

July 18, 1978

Each of us has his own rhythm of suffering.

Mourning *July 20, 1978*

Impossibility—indignity, actually—of entrusting to a drug—on the pretext of depression—my suffering, as if it were a disease, a "possession"—an alienation (something that makes you alien)—whereas it's an essential, an intimate part of yourself . . .

July 21, 1978

Mehioula.—After feeling sick through and through (to the point of advancing the date of my return), I found at M a sort of peace and even happiness: the depression is yielding. I then realize what it is I cannot tolerate: worldliness, the world, even when it's exotic (Moulay Bou Selham, Casablanca) and what it is I need: *a gentle exile*: an absence of world (*my* world) without solitude (even at El Jadida, where I ran into friends, I felt less well than I do here); here I have only Moka, whose conversation I have great difficulty understanding (though he talks to me a lot), his lovely, silent wife, his wild kids, the available boys of the Oued, Angel who brings me an enormous bouquet of lilies and yellow gladiolas, and the dogs (incidentally, a terrible racket at night), etc.

Mourning *July 24, 1978*
Mehioula

In every trip, finally, that cry—each time I think of her: *I want to return*—though I know she's not there waiting for me.

(Returning where she is absent?—where nothing foreign, nothing indifferent, reminds me she's no longer there.)

[Already here at Mehioula, where I've been so close to an endurable solitude, where I've felt the best of all my trips, here, as soon as the "world" shows its nose (friends from Casablanca, a small radio, friends from El Jadida, etc.), I felt nowhere near so well.]

Mehioula
July 24, 1978

Last day at M.

Morning. Sunshine, a bird with a special, rather literary song, country noises (a motor), solitude, peace, no aggression.

And yet—more than ever, in this *pure* air, I begin crying when I think of *maman*'s words that always lacerate me: my R! my R! (I've never been able to tell this to anyone).

Mourning *July 24, 1978*

What *maman* has given me: *regularity in the body*: not the Law but a Rule (Effectiveness but very little availability).

or Φ [1]

Photo of the Winter Garden: I search desperately to find the obvious meaning.

(Photo: powerless to say what is obvious. The birth of literature)

"Innocence": which will never do harm.

1. Symbol for the word *photograph*, which Barthes employs frequently in his preparatory notes for *Camera Lucida*.

[Last night, July 26, 1978, back from Casablanca, dinner with friends. In the restaurant (Pavillon du Lac), Paul disappears; JL thinks it's because of some sort of quarrel they've had. In his distress he leaves to try to find Paul, returns in a sweat, agonized, blaming himself—recalls suicidal attempts Paul has threatened, leaves again, looking for him in the park, etc.]

General discussion. How can anyone know? P is crazy (happening) or cruel (I say—meaning: *rude*) (Always this problem of insanity).

→ And I think: Maman *taught me you cannot make someone you love suffer.*

She never made anyone she loved suffer. That was her definition, her "*innocence.*"

Bibliothèque Nationale *July 29*

Bonnet 29[1]

Letter from Proust to André Beaunier after his mother's death, 1906.

Proust explains that he could be happy only in his misery . . . (but feels guilty for having been, for his mother, because of his own poor health, the cause of anxiety) "If such a thought did not continually lacerate me, I would find in memory, in survival, in the perfect communion in which we lived an unknown sweetness"

—p. 31. Letter to Georges de Lauris, whose mother has just died (1907).

"Now there is one thing I can tell you: you will enjoy certain pleasures you would not fathom now. When you still had your mother you often thought of the days when you would have her no longer. Now you will often think of days past when you had her. When you are used to this horrible thing that they will forever be cast into the past, then you will gently feel her revive, returning to take her place, her entire place, beside you. At the present time, this is not yet possible. Let yourself be inert,

1. Henri Bonnet, *Marcel Proust de 1907 à 1914*, Nizet, 1971.

wait till the incomprehensible power (. . .) that has broken you restores you a little, I say a little, for henceforth you will always keep something broken about you. Tell yourself this, too, for it is a kind of pleasure to know that you will never love less, that you will never be consoled, that you will constantly remember more and more."

July 29, 1978

(Saw a Hitchcock film, *Under Capricorn*)

Ingrid Bergman (around 1946): I don't know why, nor how to express it: this actress, this actress's body moves me, touches something in me which reminds me of *maman*: her complexion, her lovely, simple hands, an impression of freshness, a non-narcissistic femininity . . .

Paris, July 31, 1978

I live in my suffering and that makes me happy.

Anything that keeps me from living in my suffering is unbearable to me.

July 31, 1978

I ask for nothing but to live in my suffering.

August 1, 1978

[Perhaps already noted]

Always (painfully) surprised to be able—finally—to live with my suffering, which means that it is literally *endurable*. But—no doubt—this is because I can, more or less (in other words, with the feeling of not managing to do so) utter it, put it into words. My culture, my taste for writing gives me this apotropaic or *integrative* power: I *integrate*,* by language.

My suffering is *inexpressible* but all the same *utterable*, speakable. The very fact that language affords me the word "intolerable" immediately achieves a certain tolerance.

*enter into a whole—federate—socialize, communize, gregoriate.

August 1, 1978

Disappointment of various places and trips. Not really comfortable anywhere. Very soon, this cry: *I want to go back!* (but where? since she is no longer anywhere, who was once where I *could go back*). I am seeking my place. *Sitio.*

August 1, 1978

Which is what literature is: that I cannot read without pain, without choking on truth, everything Proust writes in his letters about sickness, courage, the death of his mother, his suffering, etc.

August 1, 1978

Horrible figure of mourning: acedia, hard-heartedness: irritability, impotence to love. Anguished because I don't know how to restore generosity to my life—or love. How to love?

—Closer to the Mother of Bernanos's *Country Priest* than to the Freudian schema.

—How I loved *maman*: I never resisted going to meet her, celebrated seeing her again (vacations), put her within my "freedom"; in short I *associated* her profoundly, scrupulously. Acedia comes from such desolation: no one, around me, for whom I would have the courage to do the same thing. Desolating egoism.

August 1, 1978

Mourning. At the death of the loved being, acute phase of narcissism: one emerges from sickness, from servitude. Then, gradually, freedom takes on a leaden hue, desolation settles in, narcissism gives way to a sad egoism, an absence of generosity.

August 3, 1978

Occasionally (for instance, yesterday, in the courtyard of the Bibliothèque Nationale), how to express that fleeting thought that *maman* is *never* again to be here; a sort of black wing (of the definitive) passes over me and chokes my breathing; a pain so acute that it seems as if, in order to survive, I must immediately drift toward something else.

August 3, 1978

Exploration of my (apparently vital) need of solitude: and yet I have a (no less vital) need of my friends.

I must therefore: 1) force myself to "call" them from time to time, find the energy to do so, combat my—telephonic (among other kinds)—apathy; 2) ask them to understand that above all they must let me call them. If they less often, less systematically, got in touch with me, that would mean for me that I must get in touch with them.

Make no trips except those during which I have no time to say: *I want to go back!*

August 10, 1978
Proust SB 87[1]

"Beauty is not like a superlative of what we imagine, a sort of abstract type we have before our eyes, but on the contrary a new, unimaginable type that reality affords us."

[Similarly: my suffering is not like the superlative of pain, of abandonment, etc., a sort of abstract type (which could be recovered by metalanguage), but on the contrary a new type, etc.]

1. Marcel Proust, *Contre Sainte-Beuve*, Gallimard, 1954. The pagination Barthes uses is that of the paperback edition (Idées Gallimard, 1965).

August 10, 1978

Proust, *Contre Sainte-Beuve,* 146
On his mother:
. . . "and the lovely lines of her countenance . . . , deeply stamped with Christian sweetness and Jansenist [Protestant][1] courage . . ."

1. Barthes added the bracketed word "Protestant," his mother's faith.

(August 10, 1978)
Sainte-Beuve, 356

"Both of us kept silence."

Agonizing pages on Proust's separation from his mother:

"But if I were gone for months, for years, for . . ."

"Both of us kept silence . . . etc."

and: "I said: forever. But that evening (. . .) the souls are immortal and will one day be reunited . . .

(August 10, 1978)

Struck by the fact that Jesus loved Lazarus and that before resuscitating him, he wept (John 11).

"Lord, behold, he whom thou lovest is sick."

"When he had heard therefore that he was sick, he abode two days still in the same place where he was."

"Our friend Lazarus sleepeth; but I go, that I may awake him out of sleep." [resuscitate him]

". . . he groaned in the spirit and was troubled, etc."

11, 35 "Lord, come and see." Jesus wept. Then said the Jews, "Behold how he loved him!"

Jesus therefore again groaning in himself . . .

(August 10, 1978)

[Proust's portrait of Robert de Flers's grandmother, who had just died (*Chroniques*, p. 72[1])

"I who had seen *her tears of a grandmother—her tears of a little girl*— . . .]

1. Marcel Proust, *Chroniques*, Gallimard, 1927. The text alluded to is entitled "Une grand'mère" and appeared in *Le Figaro* (July 23, 1927). The italics are Barthes's, but the page reference is incorrect: actually it should be pages 67–68.

August 11, 1978

Leafing through an album of Schumann, I immediately recalled that *maman* had loved his Intermezzi (on a record I once played for her).

Maman: few words between us, I remained silent (a phrase of La Bruyère, cited by Proust), but I remember every one of her tastes, of her judgments.

August 12, 1978

(Haiku. Munier. p. xxii)[1]

Calm weekend of August 15; while the radio is broadcasting Bartok's *Wooden Prince,* I'm reading this (in the visit to the Kashino Temple, the long account of Bashō's journey): "We remained sitting for a long interval in extreme silence."

Immediately I feel a sort of satori, mild, felicitous, as if my grief were being soothed, sublimated, reconciled, deepening without abating—as if "I were recovering myself."

1. Roger Munier, *Haiku,* Fayard, Documents spirituels, 1978.

August 18, 1978

Why is it that I no longer bear traveling? Why is it that I keep trying, like a lost child, to "get back home"—though *maman* is no longer there?

Continuing to "speak" to *maman* (shared language being a kind of presence) is not affected by internal discourse (I have never "talked" to her that way), but in my way of life: I try to continue living day by day according to her values: to recover something of the nourishment she provided by producing it myself, her household order, that alliance of ethics and aesthetics that was her incomparable fashion of living, of constructing the quotidian. Now, that "personality" of household empiricism is not possible while traveling—is possible only at home. To travel is to separate myself from her—still more now that she is no longer there—that she is no more than the most intimate expression of the quotidian.

August 18, 1978

The locality of the room where she was sick, where she died, and where I now live, the wall against which the head of her bed rested where I have placed an icon—not out of faith—and still put flowers on a table next to it. I have reached the point of no longer wanting to travel in order to be here, so that the flowers here will always be fresh.

August 18, 1978

To share the *values* of the silent dailiness (to manage the cooking, the cleaning, the clothes, the choice and something like the past of objects), this was my (silent) way of conversing with her. —And this is, her no longer being here, how I can still do it.

August 21, 1978

Actually the common feature of my depressions, of the moments when *I am down* (trips, social situations, certain aspects of Urt, crypto-amorous requirements), would be this: that I cannot bear what—even by relay—I might take for a *substitute* for *maman*.

And where it proceeds least badly is when I'm in a situation where there is a sort of *extension* of my life with her (the apartment).

August 21, 1978

Why would I want the slightest posterity, the least wake, since the beings whom I have loved and love most will leave none, neither I nor a few former survivors? What would it matter for me to outlive myself in History's cold and mendacious unknown, since the memory of *maman* will not outlive me and those who have known her and who will one day die in their turn? I would not want a "monument" for myself alone.

August 21, 1978

Suffering is a form of egoism.

I speak only of myself. I am not talking about her, saying what she was, making an overwhelming portrait (like the one Gide made of Madeleine).

(Yet: everything is true: the sweetness, the energy, the nobility, the kindness.)

August 21, 1978

What seems to me the furthest from, the most antipathetic to my suffering: reading the newspaper *Le Monde* and its acid and well-informed tactics.

August 21, 1978

Trying to explain to JL (but all it takes is a sentence):

All my life, since childhood, I've had *a pleasure* to be with *maman.* This was not a habit. I would delight in the vacations at U. (although I have little use for the country-side) because I knew that I would be spending all my time with her.

September 13, 1978

The grim
egoism (egotism)
of mourning
of suffering

My Morality[1]

—The courage of discretion

—It is courageous not to be courageous

1. This entry is not dated and is crossed out.

September 17, 1978

Since *maman*'s death, despite—or because of—it, a strenuous effort to set up a grand project of writing, a gradual alteration of confidence in myself—in what I write.

(October 3, 1978)

The profound modesty she had—that made her possess, not no belongings at all (no asceticism), but very few belongings—as if she wanted, at her death, that there would be no "getting rid of" what had belonged to her.

(October 3, 1978)

(How) long everything becomes, without her.

October 6, 1978

[This afternoon, exhausting plethora of delayed chores. My lecture at the Collège ➔ Considerations concerning how crowded it might be ➔ Emotivity ➔ FEAR. And I discover (?) this:]

FEAR: always confirmed—and written—as a central feature in my case. Before *maman*'s death, this Fear: fear of losing her.

And now that I've lost her?

I'm always in FEAR, and perhaps even worse, for, paradoxically still more fragile (hence my insistence on *withdrawal*, in other words, discovering a place completely protected from Fear).

—Fear, then, but of what, now?—Of dying myself? Yes, most likely—But, apparently, less—I feel this—for dying is what *maman* has done (benevolent ghost of: joining her)

—Hence, actually: Winnicott's psychotic, *I fear a catastrophe that has already occurred.* I constantly perpetuate it in myself under a thousand substitutions.

—Hence, on the dot, a whole response of thoughts, of decisions.

—Exorcise this Fear by going *where I'm afraid to go* (places easy to determine, thanks to the signal of emotivity).

—Liquidate without interruption what prevents me, separates me from writing the text about *maman*: the active departure of Suffering: accession of Suffering to the Active position.

[Text that should finish on this note, on this overture (delivery, defection) of Fear.]

(October 7, 1978)

I reproduce in myself—I observe that I reproduce in myself minute features of *maman*: I forget—my keys, or some fruit bought in the market.

Failures of memory that supposedly *characterized* her (according to her modest complaints on this subject) now become mine.

October 8, 1978

As for death, *maman*'s death gave me the (previously quite abstract) certainty that all men are mortal—that there would never be any discrimination—and the certainty of having to die *by that logic* soothed me.

October 20, 1978

The day of the anniversary of *maman*'s death is approaching. I fear, increasingly, as if on this day (October 25) she will have to die a second time.

October 25

The anniversary of *maman*'s death.
The day at Urt.

Urt, the empty house, the cemetery, the new grave (too high, too massive for her, at the end so tiny); my heart does not swell; I feel dry, with no supporting inwardness. The symbolism of the anniversary means nothing to me.

October 25, 1978

I brood over Tolstoy's story *Father Sergius* (recently saw the bad film). In the final episode he finds peace (Meaning, or Exemption from Meaning) when he encounters a little girl as she was in his childhood now become a grandmother, Mavra, who simply concerns herself with the family she loves, without raising any problem of *appearance*, of sanctity, of the Church, etc. I tell myself: that's *maman*. She never employs a metalanguage, a pose, a deliberate image. That's what "Sanctity" is.

[O the paradox: I, so "intellectual," at least accused of being so, I so ridden by an incessant metalanguage (which I defend), she offers me in the highest degree her nonlanguage.]

FURTHER DIARY PAGES

November 4, 1978–September 15, 1979

November 4, 1978

These journal notes grow rarer. Silting up. So forgetting is inexorable? (a passing "sickness"?) And yet . . .

The high seas of suffering—leave the shores, nothing in sight. Writing is no longer possible.

November 22, 1978

Cocktail party yesterday to celebrate my 25 years at Editions du Seuil. Many friends—Are you pleased?—Yes, of course [*but* I miss *maman*].

Any "sociability" reinforces the vanity of the world in which she no longer exists.

I have, continually, "a heavy heart."

That laceration, very intense today, on this gray morning, came to me, as I think of it, from the image of Rachel, sitting somewhat apart last evening, happy about this cocktail party where she had spoken a little to various guests, dignified, "in her place," as women no longer are, and with reason, since they no longer desire a place—the rare sort of lost dignity that *maman* had (she was there, with an absolute kindness, for everyone, and yet "in her place.")

(December 4, 1978)

I write my suffering less and less yet it grows all the stronger, shifting to the realm of the eternal, since I no longer write it.

December 15, 1978

Against a background of distress, of panic (torment, duties, literary spite), a rising lump in the throat.

1) Many here love me, stand with me, but no one is *strong*: all (we're all) crazy, neurotic—not to mention the remote ones like RH. Only *maman* was strong, because she was intact against all neurosis, all madness.

2) I am writing my course and manage to write *My Novel.* And then I think with a certain laceration of one of *maman*'s last utterances: *Mon Roland! Mon Roland!* I feel like crying.

[No doubt I will be unwell, until I write something *having to do with her* (*Photo*, or something else).]

December 22, 1978

If only I could utter the *profound* desire of self-communion, of withdrawal, of "Don't concern yourself with me," which comes to me straight and inflexibly from the somehow "eternal" suffering—a self-communion so *true* that the inevitable little struggles, the caricatures, the wounds, everything that inevitably occurs as soon as one *survives*, are nothing but a bitter froth on the surface of a deep sea . . .

December 23, 1978

Little disappointments, attacks, threats, worries, sense of failure, dark times, heavy burden to carry, "penal servitude," etc. I can't help putting all that in relation to *maman*'s death. It's not that (simple magic) she's no longer here to protect me, my work was always concretely kept away from her;—but rather—or is it the same thing? that now I'm reduced to *initiating myself to the world*—a harsh initiation. Miseries of a birth.

December 29, 1978

There continues undiminished the acedia, the heartfelt bitterness, the propensity to jealousies, etc.: everything that in my heart keeps me from loving myself.

Period of self-devaluation (classical mechanism of mourning).

How to recover *equanimity*?

December 29, 1978

Having received yesterday the photo I've had reproduced of *maman* as a little girl in the Winter Garden of Chennevières, I try to keep it in front of me, on my work table. But it's too much—intolerable—too painful. This image enters into conflict with all the ignoble little combats of my life. The image is really a measure, a judge (I understand now how a photo can be sanctified, how it can guide → it's not the *identity* that is recalled, it's, within that identity, a rare *expression*, a "virtue").

December 31, 1978

Suffering is enormous, but its effect on me (for suffering: not in itself: a series of indirect *effects*) is a sort of alluvium, rust, or mud deposited on my heart: a *bitterness* of heart (irritabilities, annoyances, jealousies, lack of affection).

→ Oh what a contradiction: by *maman*'s loss I become the contrary of what she was. I want to live according to her value and reach only the contrary.

January 11, 1979

. . . the pain of never again resting my lips on those cool and wrinkled cheeks . . .

[That's banal
—Death, Suffering are nothing but: banal]

January 11, 1979

Always that painful sensation that the obligations, the people, the demands, etc. separate me from *maman.* —I long for "March 10," not to be on vacation but to recover an availability inhabited by her.

January 17, 1979

Gradually the effect of absence grows sharper: having no desire to *construct* anything new (except in writing); no friendship, no love, etc.

January 18, 1979

Since *maman*'s death, no desire to "construct" anything—except in writing. Why? Literature = the only region of Nobility (as *maman* was noble).

January 20, 1979

Maman's photo as a little girl, in the distance—in front of me on my desk. It was enough for me to look at it, to apprehend the *suchness* of her being (which I struggle to describe) in order to be reinvested by, immersed in, invaded, inundated by her goodness.

January 30, 1979

We don't forget,
but something *vacant* settles in us.

February 22, 1979

What separates me from *maman* (from the mourning that was my identification with her) is the density (enlarging, gradually accumulating) of the time when, since her death, I have been able to live without her, inhabit the apartment, work, go out, etc.

March 7, 1979

Why I cannot fasten myself, adhere to certain works, certain beings; for example, JMV. It's because my infused *values* (aesthetic and ethical) come to me from *maman*. What she loved (what she did not love) formed my values.

March 9, 1979

Maman and poverty; her struggle, her misfortunes, her courage. A kind of epic without the heroic attitude.

March 15, 1979

Only I know what my road has been for the last year and a half: the economy of this motionless and anything but spectacular mourning that has kept me unceasingly separate by its demands; a separation that I have ultimately always projected to bring to a close by a book—Stubbornness, secrecy.

March 18, 1979

Last night, bad dream. Scene with *maman*. Argument, pain, sobs: I was separated from her by something (a decision on her part?) *spiritual*. Her decision also concerned Michel. She was inaccessible.

March 18, 1979

Each time I dream about her (and I dream only of her), it is in order to see her, believe her to be alive, but other, separate.

March 29, 1979[1]

I live without any concern for posterity, no desire to be read later on (except financially, for M.), complete acceptance of vanishing utterly, no desire for a "monument"—but I cannot endure that this should be the case for *maman* (perhaps because she has not written and her memory depends entirely on me).

1. The writing of *Camera Lucida* begins after this date; at the book's end, the dates of the text's composition are noted: "April 15–June 3, 1979."

May 1, 1979

I was not *like* her, since I did not die with (at the same time as) her.

June 18, 1979
Back from Greece

Since *maman*'s death, my life has not managed to constitute itself as *memory*. Flat, without the vibratory halo of "I remember . . ."

July 22, 1979

All the "rescues" of the Project[1] have failed. I find myself with nothing to do, without any work ahead of me—except for the repeated tasks of routine. Any form of the Project: limp, nonresistant, weak coefficient of energy. "What's the use?"

—It's as if now occurred quite clearly (previously delayed by successive denials) the solemn impact of mourning on any possibility of creating a work of any kind.

A major trial, an adult trial, mourning's central, decisive trial.

1. This most likely refers to *Vita Nova*; cf. note for November 30, 1977, on page 74.

August 13, 1979

Leaving Urt, after a difficult stay, in the train near Dax (that South-West sunlight,[1] which has accompanied my life), in desperate straits, tears over *maman*'s death.

1. Cf. Barthes's article "La lumière du Sud-Ouest," published in *L'Humanité*, September 10, 1977, and reprinted in *Incidents*, Le Seuil, 1987. This article was published in English as "The Light of the Sud-Ouest" (*Incidents*, University of California Press, 1992).

(August 19, 1979)

How did *maman*, while giving us an internalized law (image of a nobility), leave us (M and me) accessible to desire, to an interest in things: the contrary of "the radical, intimate, harsh, and incessant *boredom*" that prevented Flaubert from enjoying anything and filled his soul to bursting.

September 1, 1979

Return from Urt by plane.

Still as intense but mute, grief, suffering . . . ("My R, my R").

—I am unhappy, sad at Urt.

—Then am I happy in Paris? No, that is the trap. The contrary of a thing is not its contrary, etc.

I left a place where I was unhappy and that did not make me happy to leave it.

September 1, 1979

I cannot, symbolically, abstain from visiting, during each stay at Urt, upon arrival and at departure, *maman*'s grave. But once there, I have no idea what to do. Pray? What does that mean? What content? Simply the fugitive sketch of the assumption of a position of interiority. So I leave immediately each time

(moreover the graves of this cemetery, though rural, are so ugly . . .).

September 1, 1979

Suffering; impossibility of being comfortable anywhere; oppression, irritations and remorse one after the next, everything under the sign "wretchedness of man," used by Pascal.

September 2, 1979

Nap. Dream: *exactly* her smile.
Dream: complete, successful, memory.

September 15, 1979

There are mornings so sad . . .

SOME UNDATED FRAGMENTS

[after *maman*'s death]

Painfully, the incapacity, henceforth—to become *agitated* . . .

•

Suicide

How would I know I don't suffer any more, if I'm dead?

•

In the imagination I might have of my death (which everyone has), I added to the anguish of disappearing soon the equal anguish of the *unendurable* pain I would cause her.

•

On the infrequency—the insignificance of our verbalization, of our speech: yes, but never a platitude, a stupidity—a blunder . . .

•

"Nature"

Though she did not grow up in the country, among country people, how she loved "Nature," in other words, the Natural—without any of the gestures of Anti-Pollution, which were not of her generation. She felt comfortable in somewhat tangled gardens, etc.

SOME NOTES ON *MAMAN*

March 11, 1979

FMB is very eager for me to meet Hélène de Wendel, as a woman (of the world) of exceptionally delicacy, etc. I have no interest in doing so, because:

—of course I am eager to encounter delicacy in people I am introduced to, but at the same time I know that *maman* had no interest in that world, or in that sort of women. Her delicacy was absolutely atopic (socially): exclusive of classes; without insignia.

•

April 15, 1977

The morning nurse speaks to *maman* as if she were a child, in a voice a little too loud, inquisitorial, scolding, and inane. She does not realize that *maman* is *judging her*.

[Stupidity]

People never speak of a mother's *intelligence*, as if that would diminish her affectivity, distance her as a mother. But intelligence is everything that permits us to live superlatively with another person.

•

—*Maman* and religion

—Never verbalized.

—An attachment (but what kind of attachment?) to the Bayonne community

—Kindness to minorities?

—Nonviolence

•

June 7, 1978

Christianity: the Church: yes, we were quite opposed to it when associated with the State, with Power, with Colonialism, with the Bourgeoisie, etc.

But just the other day, a sort of evidence, of what I mean: *deep down* . . . Is this part of it? And is it not within the circle of ideologies, of moralities, the one place where you can still conceive *nonviolence*?

Yet there remains for me a clear separation from Faith (and of course from Sin). But is such a thing important? A Faith without violence (without militarism, without proselytism)?

Christians: the triumphant ones become dropouts (yes, but USA? Carter, etc.).

The Aldo Moro case: better than a martyr, not a hero: a dropout.

•

Form of discretion:

to do things oneself, not to have them done by others

empirical self-sufficiency

affective link

•

How the loved being is a *relay*, establishes the major choices in affect.

Why fascism horrifies me.

Mediatrix

I never understood *where* militarism was established—the ideas, etc.

the strength of ideas (since for me, a sceptic, not an instance of truth).

My relation to violence.

Why I never accept the justifications (and even perhaps the *truth*) of violence: because I cannot (could not: but now that she's gone, it's the same thing) endure (*unendurable*) the harm that would be done to her by a violence of which I was the object.

•

Maman talking: all that, Argentina, Argentinian fascism, the poisonings, political tortures, etc.?

She would have been wounded. And I imagine her with horror among the wives and mothers of the disappeared who parade here and there. How she would have suffered if she had lost me.

•

Total (absolute) presence

absolute

weightless

density, not weight

•

To begin:

"All the time I lived with her—all my life—my mother never made *an observation* about me."

•

Maman never made an *observation* about me—Therefore I cannot endure them.

(see FW's letter)

•

Maman: (all her life): space without aggression, without meanness—She never made an *observation* about me (my horror of that word and of the thing).

•

(June 16, 1978)

A woman I hardly know and whom I am to visit telephones me (disturbs me, corners me) to no purpose, to tell me: get off at this bus stop, be careful crossing, won't you stay to dinner, etc.

Never has my mother ever said anything like all that. She has never spoken to me as if to an irresponsible child.

•

Hendaye

Not very happy
it was an *inheritance*.

AFTERWORD

Before helicopter service between the Pan Am Building and Idlewild Airport (as it was rather pastorally known in those pre-assassination days) proved to be a menace to pedestrian traffic in the streets around Grand Central Terminal for reasons of mechanical, not aeronautical, failure (a hunk of fuselage, if I remember correctly, fell onto Park Avenue just opposite the Four Seasons restaurant), my friend Roland Barthes, who was teaching for a couple of terms at Johns Hopkins University, invited his mother, with whom he lived in Paris, to join him in New York City for the Christmas holidays.

Inconveniently, Roland would not yet be released from his academic duties in Baltimore at the time of her arrival, but he assured me that even though his mother and I had not yet met, I would certainly prove a satisfactory (Roland's word was *idéal*) surrogate for her son—after all, I lived in Manhattan, I spoke French, I too had a mother. Our plan, eagerly consented to, was for Madame Barthes, by no means a seasoned traveler, to arrive by Air France at Idlewild, where we would meet in the Helicopter Lounge—Roland had insistently described each of us to the other (were we equally convinced?) as *facilement reconnaissable*—whence we would share our maiden helicopter flight to the Pan Am Building in Gotham—magical destination!—where I would take her to a "characteristic" dinner and then escort her to a midtown hotel, in fact the Hotel Gotham, where my mother always stayed during her frequent visits from Cleveland.

So, on a winter evening in 1967, once Roland's mother and I had indeed easily recognized each other (I believe the ease was entirely on her side, though I never discovered the secret of my old friend's *code amical* concerning myself; for all my subsequent lunches at their *ménage*, neither Roland nor his mother ever came clean), we shared the thrill of that prompt but glistening descent right into the towering heart of Manhattan, so much more literally, as Madame Barthes observed, *la ville lumière* than the one she had just left behind her. As we soared past the glowing towers that seemed not so much to scrape but, at twilight, rather to caress the sky, Madame Barthes, who had not seen New York City since 1904 (after a steamer crossing, of course), remarked without surprise that "*évidemment* there had been many changes in the interval."

Several times, during ensuing family lunches that included Roland, his mother and his half-brother, myself, and of course Lux, the family spaniel (if I remember the cast and the breed correctly), when I perhaps morbidly mentioned that *our* helicopter had suspended its eventually untrustworthy *va-et-vient*, Madame Barthes would remark that it was not *we* who had had a narrow escape but the reprehensible pedestrians on the ground, though *there*, she cheerfully concluded, was where she was entirely more likely to be found for the rest of her life.

This is perhaps the proper place to refer to the third general remark I ever heard Madame Barthes make; she knew, certainly, that I had translated a good number of her son's writings, but her curiosity about such an enterprise was rather roundabout. "*Monsieur Ovare,*" she asked—perhaps on that initial shared flight of ours, providing a sort of civil discourse, "what would you say the translator needs . . . oh, not to translate someone like my son's books, but as a general rule?" I knew one translator who needed everything, but before I could answer, Madame Barthes continued: "I always hear people say *a talent for languages,* but I don't think so . . . Isn't it rather that what the translator needs is *talent*?"

As the reader discovers, Roland Barthes's *Mourning Diary* is in fact a diary only in a rather desperate sense: the writer kept a stack of quartered typing paper on his desk, and from the day of his mother's death until nearly his own, while he was producing his last, best books, he would scribble one or another or sometimes several of these aphoristic losses as a sort of diagnostic test, a questioning of torment, a preparation for the day's task: the companion to the ultimate writings of Roland Barthes. It became, this multiplication of *feuilles*, a realization that yet another kind of utterance might, eventually, be constituted out of this deprivation, this dispossession, this travail; such a book was never written, but the notes toward a notation of bereavement remind us forever of what might have *come to pass*.

I believe that after Roland Barthes's death, his friends and his publisher's advisers determined, after some very powerful impulses to resist, to evade, to ignore these agonized markings altogether, instead chose to publish *Mourning Diary* as evidence of creative intention. I don't suppose Roland would have abounded in their sense, neither do I suppose he would have repudiated the enterprise. I am glad, by translating *Mourning Diary*, to indicate my agreement with those friends and advisers. Having known Madame Barthes, even provisionally, clarified for me her son's intentions neither to bury his mother nor to praise her, but to exalt her exceptional contribution to his own happiness and belief in the worthiness of life itself by the testimony of her own. Perhaps this is the task of every son, usually acknowledged by pretermission. I here recognize the task in its most veracious form, though in this instance necessarily fragmentary, of what ancient Romans called filial piety, completed by the simultaneous production of *A Lover's Discourse* and of *Roland Barthes by Roland Barthes* and all the other writings that succeed (in the true senses of that verb) his mother's death. *Mourning Diary* can be correctly read only by a concomitant reading of these ultimate books and of the hundreds of pages of Barthes's final texts written at the same time (*à la fois*) he was producing these crucial and painful notations.

And to add the inevitable personal note, *Mourning Diary,* even fragmentary, even translated, even betrayed by divulgation, is like those towers Madame Barthes and I saw perhaps scraping or even caressing the sky, but in an effort to make something, to explain something, to warrant something. Some of Barthes's friends have observed that no mother could possibly be that perfected a being, a life force and in death a paradigm, a phoenix. I wanted to translate *Mourning Diary, improbable creation though it is,* as evidence—as so many writings of Barthes testify so much more flawlessly—to the contrary.

—Richard Howard